Dholes

Victoria Blakemore

Copyright info/picture credits

Cover, Vinod Pillai/Shutterstock; Page 3, Esmeralda Edenberg/Shutterstock; Page 5, Nimit Virdi/Shutterstock; Page 7, Takashi/AdobeStock; Page 9, Dario Bajurin/Adobestock; Pages 10-11, quickshooting/AdobeStock; Page 13, Eric Gevaert/Shutterstock; Page 15, Sea_Monkey/AdobeStock; Page 17, Lifebychris/Shutterstock; Page 19, Esmeralda Edenberg/Shutterstock; Page 21, Esmeralda/AdobeStock; Page 23; NaturesMomentsuk/Shutterstock; Page 25, Mathias Appel/flickr; Page 27, subinpumsom/AdobeStock; Page 29, Anuradha Marwah/Shutterstock; Page 31, Lab_Photo/AdobeStock; Page 33, Vinod Pillai/Shutterstock

Table of Contents

What Are Dholes?

Dholes [DOHLS] are a kind of wild dog. They are also called Asiatic wild dogs, whistling dogs, and red dogs.

They are members of the **Canidae** family. Other members of this family include wolves, foxes, coyotes, and jackals.

Dholes are red, brown, tan, black, and white in color. They often have a white belly and black tip on their tail.

Size

Dholes often grow to be about three feet in length. Their tail can add up to eighteen inches to their length. They usually stand about twenty inches tall at the shoulder.

When fully grown, they often weigh between twenty-two and forty-four pounds.

Female dholes are usually smaller than male dholes.

Physical Characteristics

Dholes have a shorter, thicker muzzle than many other large dogs. They also have fewer **molars** than other dogs.

They have long, strong legs. They use their strong legs to run and jump when catching their prey.

The color of a dhole's fur can often be used as **camouflage**. It helps dholes to blend in with their habitat.

Habitat

Dholes can live in a **variety** of habitats. They are often found in meadows, jungles, and in the hills and mountains.

It is often very hot where dholes live. They like to rest in clearings or open areas during the day. They are most active early in the morning when it is cooler.

Range

Dholes are found in Asia. They are found in small groups that are far apart.

They are found in parts of countries such as China, India, and Malaysia.

Diet

Dholes are **carnivores**. They eat meat.

Their diet is made up of hoofed animals such as deer, buffalo, wild pigs, reindeer, wild sheep, and wild goats. They may also eat smaller animals such as lizards and rabbits.

When hunting alone, dholes are more likely to hunt smaller prey. This is less common than pack hunting.

Dholes usually work as a pack to hunt their prey. They use whistling sounds as they move through the **underbrush**. They often pounce on their prey from behind to catch it.

Dholes eat very fast. Two or three dholes can eat an entire deer in a few minutes.

Dholes are able to catch prey that is much larger than they are because they work together.

Communication

Dholes use sound, scent, and movement to communicate with each other. They use movements like wagging their tail or bending back their ears to send signals.

Like many predators, dholes mark their **territory** with a special scent. It tells other animals that the area is taken.

They are called whistling dogs because they have a special whistling sound they use. They can also cluck and scream to communicate.

Movement

Dholes are very **agile**. They are able to run, jump, and turn very quickly. They have been known to run at speeds of up to forty-five miles per hour.

They have been seen jumping as high as seven feet in the air. Being able to jump high and far helps them to catch their prey.

Dholes are good swimmers and
love the water. They are often
seen swimming or sitting in the
water.

Dhole Pups

Dholes usually have three or four pups in a **litter**, although they can have up to twelve at a time.

Pups are taken care of by the rest of the pack. The pack brings them food until they are old enough to join the hunt.

Pups are fully grown by the time they are one year old. They can start having their own pups by the time they are three years old.

Dhole Life

Dholes live in groups that are called packs. A pack is often made up of between five and twelve dholes.

Packs live in **burrows**. Each burrow has many different entrance. The burrows are usually taken over after other animals leave them.

Packs work together to hunt and

take care of pups. Sometimes

different packs come together

to form super packs to hunt. **23**

African Wild Dogs

Another kind of wild dog is the African wild dog. Although they are found in different areas, there are some **similarities** between the two.

Both kinds of wild dogs live and hunt together in packs. They are friendly with other wild dogs and work and play together.

African wild dogs look very

different from dholes, but they

have similar behaviors.

Population

Dholes are **endangered**. There are not many left in the wild. If their population continues to **decline**, they could become **extinct**.

Dholes are very spread out and hard to track. There are thought to be around 2,000 left in the wild, but it is not known for sure.

In the wild, dholes often live up to ten years. They can live as long as sixteen years in zoos.

Dholes in Danger

Dholes are facing many threats from humans. They are often trapped or poisoned by people who see them as **pests**. Their dens are often destroyed.

In places where people live close to dhole habitats, dholes can catch diseases from **domesticated** dogs.

Dhole habitats are being destroyed for farms, buildings, and roads. It is getting harder for them to find prey.

Helping Dholes

In some countries, special protected areas have been set up. These areas provide animals such as dholes with a safe habitat to live in.

Some groups focus on education. They teach people who live near dholes about ways they can live without **conflict**.

Researchers are studying dholes. They want to learn more about dholes so they can find new ways to help them.

Special collars are put on wild dholes to **monitor** where they go. This information will help researchers know where dholes need protection.

Glossary

Agile: moving quickly and gracefully

Camouflage: using color to blend in to the surroundings

Carnivore: an animal that eats only meat

Conflict: a disagreement or fight

Decline: get smaller

Endangered: at risk of becoming extinct

Extinct: when there are no more of an animal left in the wild

Litter: a group of animals born at the same time

Molars: large teeth found in the back of the mouth, used for grinding food

Monitor: to observe and check up on

Pests: someone or something that annoys or bothers

Similarities: ways that things are the same

Territory: an area of land that an animal claims as its own

Variety: many kinds

About the Author

Victoria Blakemore is a first grade

teacher in Southwest Florida with a

passion for reading.

You can visit her at

www.elementaryexplorers.com

Also in This Series

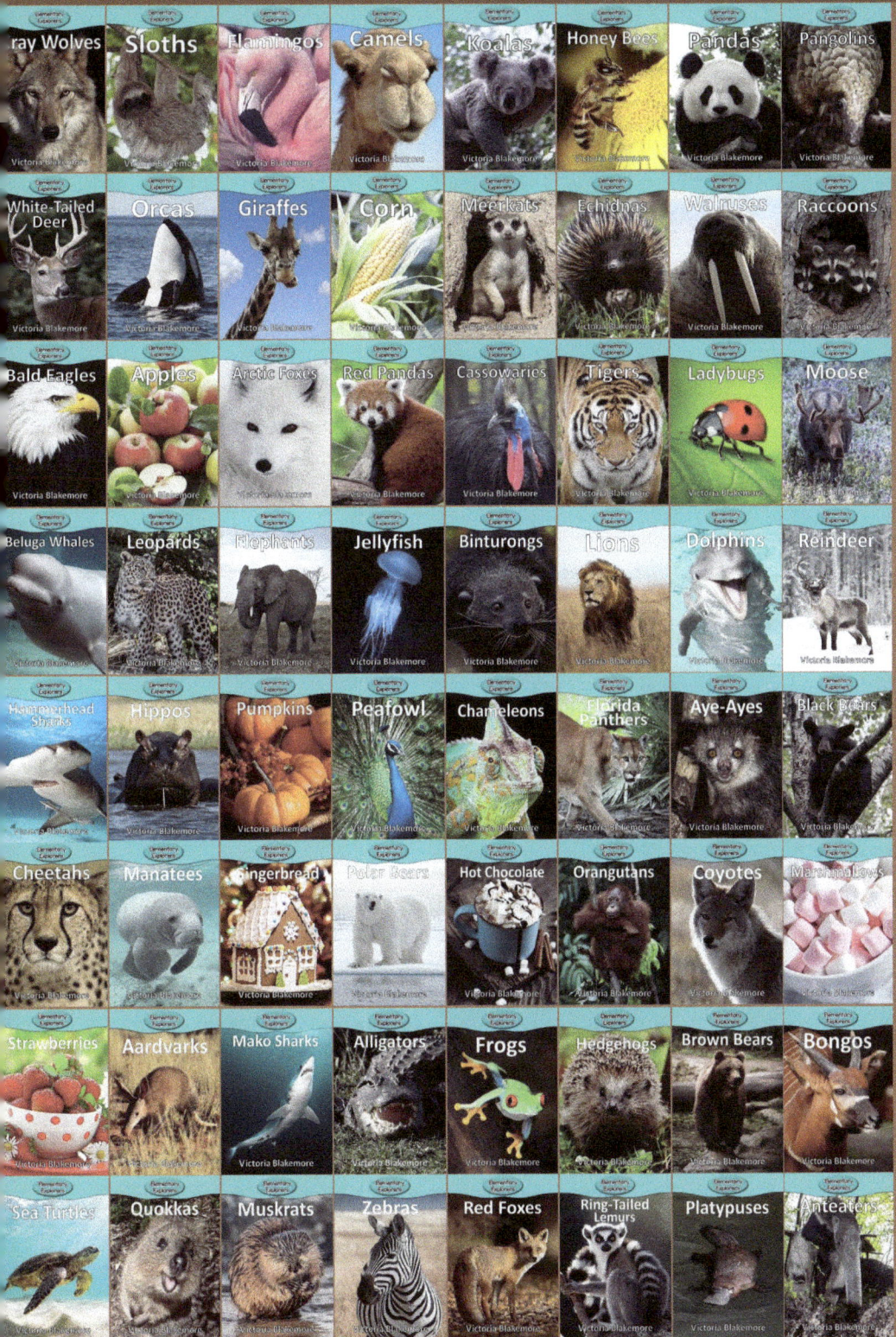

Gray Wolves · Sloths · Flamingos · Camels · Koalas · Honey Bees · Pandas · Pangolins

White-Tailed Deer · Orcas · Giraffes · Corn · Meerkats · Echidnas · Walruses · Raccoons

Bald Eagles · Apples · Arctic Foxes · Red Pandas · Cassowaries · Tigers · Ladybugs · Moose

Beluga Whales · Leopards · Elephants · Jellyfish · Binturongs · Lions · Dolphins · Reindeer

Hammerhead Sharks · Hippos · Pumpkins · Peafowl · Chameleons · Florida Panthers · Aye-Ayes · Black Bears

Cheetahs · Manatees · Gingerbread · Polar Bears · Hot Chocolate · Orangutans · Coyotes · Marshmallows

Strawberries · Aardvarks · Mako Sharks · Alligators · Frogs · Hedgehogs · Brown Bears · Bongos

Sea Turtles · Quokkas · Muskrats · Zebras · Red Foxes · Ring-Tailed Lemurs · Platypuses · Anteaters

Also in This Series

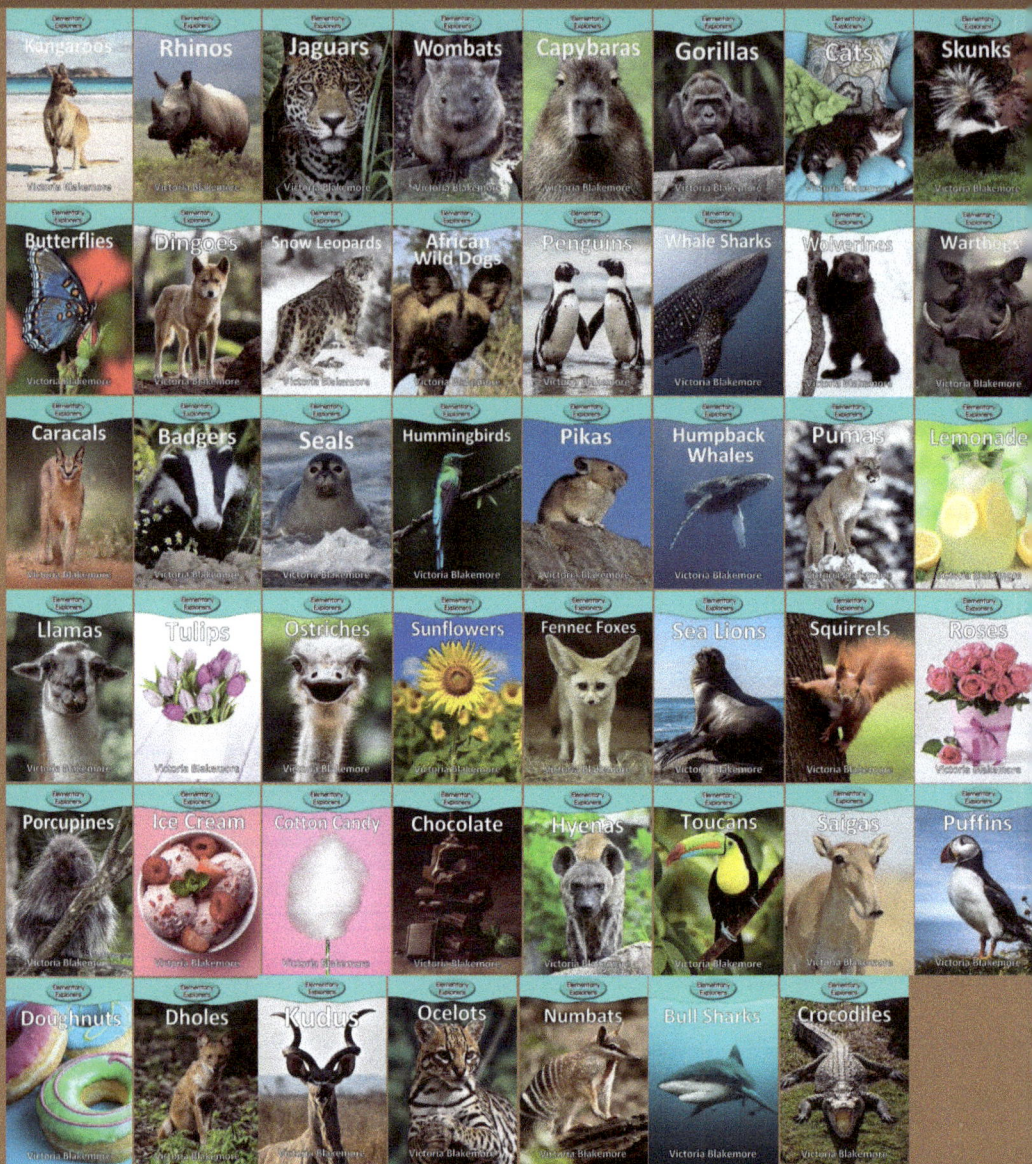

Kangaroos	Rhinos	Jaguars	Wombats	Capybaras	Gorillas	Cats	Skunks
Butterflies	Dingoes	Snow Leopards	African Wild Dogs	Penguins	Whale Sharks	Wolverines	Warthogs
Caracals	Badgers	Seals	Hummingbirds	Pikas	Humpback Whales	Pumas	Lemonade
Llamas	Tulips	Ostriches	Sunflowers	Fennec Foxes	Sea Lions	Squirrels	Roses
Porcupines	Ice Cream	Cotton Candy	Chocolate	Hyenas	Toucans	Saigas	Puffins
Doughnuts	Dholes	Kudus	Ocelots	Numbats	Bull Sharks	Crocodiles	

www.ingramcontent.com/pod-product-compliance
Lightning Source LLC
Chambersburg PA
CBHW052124030426
42335CB00025B/3109